Talk to Me!

By the Same Author

CHARLIE W. SHEDD

Talk to Me!

1975

Doubleday & Company, Inc., Garden City, New York

Library of Congress Cataloging in Publication Data

Shedd, Charlie W.

    Talk to me!
    1. Marriage. 2. Interpersonal relations.
I. Title.
HQ734.S537   301.42

ISBN 0-385-04495-X

Library of Congress Catalog Card Number 74–9465

Contents

Dear Dr. Shedd:

You've heard of the Sphinx?
Well, I married it. And I feel like I'm
living with a total stranger.

It never has been very good,
but lately it's been getting worse. Do
you know how barren it is to merely exist
with someone who makes nothing but guttural
sounds? And then only when he wants something like sex, or food, or change the
channel. That's Roger.

Is there anything a woman can do
to get her husband to communicate?

Please help me.

Heather

Heather is a beautiful name. In my book of names one of its meanings is "bell-like flower of Scotland."

That letter about the sphinx is an excerpt from a real letter. But the names have been changed, and so have all the others to follow.

I set this book in letters, because it seemed most natural in letters. My mail brings me a steady stream of correspondence. Questions from over a million readers of my books *Letters to Philip* and *Letters to Karen*. Marriage questions. And the number-one cry I hear from women is, "Why won't he talk to me?"

This is the main query too at women's seminars. Same thing at conferences, meetings, workshops where my wife and I are invited often. Always the same question surfaces. In the dialogue period, every time, this will be first on the agenda: "How can I get my husband to communicate?"

One thing I've never been is a woman whose man won't talk. But I lived with one for a time. Then, by the wonderful ways women have, she helped me open the doors inside.

She brought me to see how much better life could be transparent.

You will sense that some of the things I write are her secrets. Others are the ingenious methods of wise women we've admired.

So I write here in the hope that this book may be a personal message to you. And to any wife who qualifies for the second meaning of Heather—

"SYMBOL OF LONELINESS"

Talk to Me!

Check Your Own Output

Dear Heather,

The most beautiful marriage I know started with two lonely people.

I should know. I was one of them.

So here's the good news. There's hope for you and Roger. Many a patient wife has successfully turned her zombie into a communicator.

I like the way you put your question: "Is there anything a woman can do to get her husband talking?" Always the best place to begin making changes is at the mirror. So you are right to start with yourself.

Here's a good question for openers: Are *you* talking too much?

Sometimes we help the other person communicate when we zipper our lip. There are women, like Tennyson's brook, who go babbling on forever. Picturesque and you can almost hear it. But it's bad living for any man. And here's one way to check yourself. Whenever you're with a friend, a group, your husband—are you doing 51 per cent of the talking? If you are, somebody's sure to be bored.

Then too you might do another check on your favorite themes. Are you talking so much about your interests you're clobbering his? I've known some wives who bored their husbands stiff (literally) this way.

We have one friend who is completely gone on something called "acrostics." I hope it's only a passing fancy, because if it isn't, I see a dim future for her. There she sits alone with her acrostics while her man is with another woman. No husband will go on forever trying to relate to a one-song singer. Especially if it's not his song.

While you're checking your subjects, here's another negative. I know some women who are dull because they can't seem to talk anything but woman talk. Any man worth his manners will listen a bit to the feminine themes. But you better know it's a pretty small bit.

So it's a good idea to keep checking your subjects as well as the amount of your talk.

You'll need to know also how men are about aches and pains. If you're really hurting, of course, he should be caring. When you begin overdoing it, he'll tune you out.

So if you're smart, you'll keep studying the female monologues that turn men off. You can learn to catch yourself when you're into them. If you work at it, you can make yourself a more interesting conversationalist for Roger.

Kelly did it.

Her husband is high honcho in a major American conglomerate. Even when he's home, he's contemplating million-dollar deals. Kelly is a great conversationalist, but it hasn't always been like that. You can sense she bubbles with life and she loves to talk about it. But she also loves Joe, so she has trained herself in an unusual method for drawing him into the conversation. And she's done it so long, it's the natural thing for her now.

If you could see her at this, you'd admire her expertise. I don't know anyone better.

On a recent evening in their home the subject turned to that beautiful house they'd left behind in New England. She was describing their yard and how it sloped down to the brook. Then, just when you'd expect her to get poetic, she stopped. "Joe, you tell them, will you? I love to hear you describe it."

You think that's putting him on? I do too. But I've heard her do it with all kinds of subjects. Government. Money. Their children. Religion. Ecology. Race relations.

Every man has a touch of admiration for the right kind of smoothie. So that night when the girls went to prepare a snack, I told Joe how much we enjoyed Kelly. Made some remarks about her skill at conversation, her social graces. He grinned his big grin and then he said with pride, "Charlie, she's some kind of con artist, isn't she? And I love her for it."

So, she's a con artist! That's what Joe calls her. But I call her very wise. Which can also be said for any woman who keeps checking her output. Often.

Sorry Roger doesn't communicate. But maybe we can

do something about it. And you began at the right place when you asked: "Could it be Heather is *overcommunicating?*"

P.S. Just thought of a dandy on talking too much about the feminine themes. Junior was writing a report for Social Studies. So he went to his dad with the question, "Can you give me some good stuff on Women's Lib?"

Father (from behind the sports page): "Go ask your mother."

Junior (after serious thought, like thirty seconds): "But Dad, I didn't want to know *that* much."

Transparency

Dear Heather,

If I had to choose one word as the description of perfect marriage, this is the word—transparency. The dictionaries say it means seeing through the surface. Which for two people living together would require a mutual openness in their life style.

I believe the desire to know and be known is standard equipment on the human model. We were created for relationships. If that is true, it says something good for you and Roger. He really does want to be known. Behind the walls there is a lonely man who would like to get out.

Sure, I suppose some men are hopeless, but don't let yourself think Roger is one of them. At least, not until you've tried everything. And that may take a long time.

Transparency is a process. It doesn't happen all at once. We're still working at it after thirty-five years. And we're still discovering wonderful new things about each other.

So total transparency is a life goal. But you can have fun developing it as the years go by.

I think I hear you saying, "Sounds good. Where do we start?"

In my next letter I'll tell you about one good beginning. It's a time commitment which for us was one of the greatest things we ever did. You and Roger can do it if you're both willing. And when you decide to do it, you take one of the finest first steps for great friendship.

Time Together Alone

Dear Heather,

When Martha and I decided we really wanted to know each other, we made this deal:

Once a week we will go from our home for an old-fashioned date. Dinner together. A drive. Something we both enjoy. We will not count occasions when we are invited out or entertaining. We will not let our children, business, guests, anything rob us of this decision to become friends.

In thirty-five years of marriage that means 1,820 times we've been together in depth. Multiply that by two or three hours per date and you get the idea.

This doesn't mean eating with the family or watching television. Nothing the matter with dinnertime talk or sharing favorite TV programs. But many a husband and wife become strangers sitting side by side with the tube turned on and their hearts turned off to each other. And the same goes for lots of good stuff. Serving on committees, community efforts, P.T.A., church activities. The smart couple keeps checking to be sure the "good" isn't crowding out the "better" and the "best."

Weekends together are a fine thing, and trips. I hope you have some of these. Nice bonus. Yet "where it's at" for long-time oneness is steady staying with it.

I have no secrets for opening Roger up in a hurry. Some things can't be done in a hurry. But since the time is sure to pass anyway, why not put it to good use? One way you do this is to establish some trusts between you. Like a good trust, the more you invest, the more you will have later.

As you spend more time together, the more you will want time to communicate. So you look for more time. And the busier you are, the more you will feel the need of this deep sharing.

"When" doesn't matter really. Neither does "where." Or what you have to eat. Great soul communication is possible over hamburgers. Or pizza. Or a picnic brought from home.

We even have a nice little thing for times when we are hosting overnight guests. On those days we go out for breakfast alone. Almost always. And here's an interesting sidelight. The reaction of our guests to this practice is summed up by the lady who said, "As I sat eating my roll in your kitchen and thought about you two, I couldn't help wishing my husband and I had it like that."

Question: How do you get Roger to take the lead in this "Time Together Alone" compact?

Answer: Maybe you don't. So *you* tell him you need some time with him alone. Not once. Not now and then. Regularly. Ask him if he'll make this deal with you: one date for just the two of you, every week.

If he'll buy that on a trial basis for three months, you've hit a winner. I can promise you right now what will happen. At the end of that period, you'll both begin to feel the start of a new friendship.

I Need Your Advice

Dear Heather,

As pastor in a small Nebraska town, I got loaded up with people problems. Marital problems mostly. Husbands alone, wives alone, and sometimes they came together. Alcoholics came, and relatives trying to understand alcoholics. Unmarried girls came, pregnant. College students. High school. Junior highers. Fathers. Mothers. Couples came to get married, and others to get out of marriage. Men hating their jobs, they came too. You name it, I saw it. Over and over.

So here I was, helping all these people. I guess I was helping. At least they kept coming and they sent their friends. And their friends sent their friends. My calendar was crammed. I kid you not, this stuff got heavy.

Where does a dentist go when his teeth need fixing? I guess he goes to another dentist. So a counselor, if he needs counseling, would go to another counselor. Except in our town there were no other counselors. Which may give you some insight into why they lined up at my door. But whose door could I go to?

Meanwhile back at the bungalow, somebody else had problems. Why does a counselor think his wife can go merrily on forever?

Well, she can't, alone! And I'll never forget that night she broke the sound barrier. She fed me first. (Good idea.) Then she sat me down by the big bay window, eyeball to eyeball. "Listen," she said. "You've got to listen. I'm having an awful problem. Please, won't you listen? I need your advice."

So I listened. For the first time in a long time I tuned in to her suffering. And do you know what happened? Out of that experience we came to the realization that a husband and wife *can* counsel each other.

Now, I know Roger isn't a professional counselor. So, what if he isn't? He's very much a man. And I'll tell you this about men. Every man with normal reactions is proud that his friends and fellow workers come asking his counsel. You can count on this, Heather. There's hardly a man who won't turn on when people turn to him for help.

So how about this for your starting technique? "Roger, I've got a problem. I need your advice. Please listen."

You keep on doing that honestly. No pretending. Nothing but the real thing. You do it long enough, and I'll bet on a breakthrough.

That's what happened at our house. She never gave up. She kept on saying, "I need you." And I heard her.

Out of this came a miracle. It was the miracle of a locked-in man opening up. To listen. To share.

Say It Back

Dear Heather,

When a man begins to surface himself, what his woman does right now is crucial. Martha and I have a technique which has done a lot for us.

We call this "say it back." It simply means you repeat back to Roger what he has said to you.

This will be particularly useful when you think he's about to come up with something negative. Guilt. Anger. Worry. Any hidden feeling.

If you're like most of us, your first reaction to some of these may be negative. You'll want to return the negative in some way. You'll want to withdraw, pout, argue, let him have it.

In "say it back," before you make any comment, you simply play his record over to him.

Example:
Roger: "You contradicted me in front of the kids."

Heather: (normal reaction) "You do it too. Remember last Tuesday?" Or, "Look who's talking!"

Heather: (in "say it back") "You mean you don't like it when I put you down in front of the kids."

Roger: (if normal) "Yes, like you questioned my judgment about the importance of grades."

Heather: "You mean how I said too much emphasis is placed on scholastic achievement."

Now Roger will enlarge on what else happened in this particular situation. You keep giving it back to him with some slight variation. Go on until he gets it all out of his system.

Example #2:

Roger: "That damn Jim Case is impossible. No way I can go on working under these conditions."

Heather: (first reaction) "Oh, you're always complaining about Jim Case." Or, "Jim Case can't be that bad." Or, "No job is perfect. Everybody has it tough."

Heather: (in "say it back") "You mean Jim Case is hard to work with."

Now Roger will agree and continue. You may even discover he's worried about his future. Keep up this process until you both see the situation with new clarity. You will recognize immediately times when this could have been effective between you if you'd used it.

Can you sense what a healing process this could be? By

"say it back," you encourage the flow. You invite him to keep coming on. The more you draw his negatives out of him, the better he will feel inside. Better toward you. Better toward everyone, including those impossible people like Jim Case. You are serving as his cleanser for the ugly stuff.

We've taught "say it back" in group therapy sessions. We know from dozens of witnesses it can make a mighty difference. Here's a letter from one woman who says:

I want you to know that I had been living with a very difficult man. Now, the more I remember to "say it back," the more livable he becomes. I think he must have had so much of the bad inside him, it was coming out in his reactions to me.

Another:

My husband was drinking too much. Without saying so, we were both worried about it. Since I started "say it back," things are getting much better. Do you suppose he was trying to get some liquid rearrangement of his inner confusion? Well, whatever happened, I want to report he seems to be more in control of himself. And that's something really marvelous, because he's more like he used to be.

The reason this treatment works with a man is that it works with every normal human being. Male and female alike want to be understood. That's how our Creator put us together.

Even if Roger doesn't talk much, he has these feelings deep inside. He'd like to know that his ideas and his reactions to life make a difference somewhere. If you can be that somewhere, he'll come back to you. You represent the one spot in the world sensitive to his thoughts and feelings. You know he can't express himself totally in the business world. He wouldn't dare. But if he isn't afraid of your reaction, he's more likely to open up at home. The more he appreciates opening up at home, the more he will learn to do it right. He will develop ways of expression acceptable both to him and to you.

So run it over and over through your mind until it becomes a part of your relationship:

Say it back

Say it back

Say it back

The Pump

Dear Heather,

Only time for a quickie today. So here's a country illustration as a follow up to "say it back."

Where I grew up, there was one pump which had to be primed every time. It furnished our best drinking water. My job was to draw a bucket morning, noon, and night. There was a tin dipper hanging on the pump. And it better be used. Reason? This particular pump would give two dippers' full without priming. And that's absolutely all it would give. No more. But if you poured this back into it, you'd get water. Beautiful water. Lots of it. A bucketful. Two. Or all you needed.

So many people are like that pump. You take the little bit they give, give it back, and they'll start flowing.

"Hmmm . . ."

Dear Heather,

Do you ever catch yourself cutting Roger off before he's finished talking? I've done the same thing, especially with my family. Why do we treat the general public with our better manners and save the worst for home?

One answer is that we think we know what people are going to say, so we don't let them say it. We finish their sentences for them. We don't let them get it all out.

What's the solution? Psychologists have a term with profound meaning. It is "listening with the third ear." It calls for us to remember there are meanings behind the words. When we have heard what they say, we need to listen and listen and listen. We need to listen until we understand what they're saying and they understand it. This is what "say it back" is all about. It's an art, and when you've mastered this art, another nice thing happens. Now you can develop certain signals between you to speed up your understanding.

Example?

It's a great day in any marriage when you learn to say "Hmmm . . ." with meaning. There are numerous inflections of that profound sound. But what I refer to here is the one which says "Hmmm . . . , that's interesting. Tell me more."

Some men I know have clammed up forever. But some who appear to have clammed up are still looking. They're looking for another kind of woman. She's the one with the third ear.

"Hmmm . . ."

Why Men Die Sooner

Dear Heather,

Here's a thought from the insurance companies. I was reading recently their startling claim. They say a majority of the women now living will be widows for seven years. Some company figures go as high as eleven. And a psychiatrist tells us why this is true. "Most breadwinners can't be as honest as they'd like to be. The average man must lead a more strictured life than his woman. To bring home that check he must not speak his mind. Even when he knows the boss is wrong, he better not say it right out."

That's what the man says. My interpretation of his wordy conclusion is: Every time a man hides his true feeling, he shortens his life span. He's tightening the band a little bit tighter around his true self.

Well, if you think Roger's impossible, here is at least one thing you can do—check his insurance policies.

But if you are the gal I think you are, these figures won't

throw you. They will be all the more challenge to your ingenuity. Maybe there's a beautiful man inside Roger you've never really met. Perhaps he's exactly the right person for living to a ripe old age with you.

I Like You Because

Dear Heather,

One of the favorite stories at our house is this from *Letters to Karen:*

> An old grouch lived with his wife for twenty-one years and never spoke a single word. Then one morning at breakfast, he broke the silence with "Darling, sometimes when I think how much you mean to me, it is almost more than I can do to keep from telling you."

That's some kind of ludicrous, isn't it? Or *is* it? Whittle a few years off the tale, and you find it right on in too many homes.

Why do we shut down the flow of nice things between us? Not being a woman, I can't give you a woman's reasons. But I know this firsthand about men—often back in our masculine beginnings, we took on some erroneous notions. One of these is that tenderness is a sign of weakness.

Women can display their emotions. But men must steel themselves for the hard stuff.

"Where Have All the Flowers Gone?" no longer appears on the hit list. But the theme plays on and on in many a woman's heart.

So what does this have to do with better communication? Well, maybe a lot if you can understand this one thing further about men. We may not be good at giving compliments, but oh, boy, how we love to receive them.

Doesn't seem fair, does it? Yet this is a fact you can count on: Any man in his right mind goes big for feminine praise.

So let's get specific. In the most turned-on marriage, I know, they made a deal. Way back near the beginning they agreed to something both of them needed. Every day they would pay each other a compliment. Big compliment. Little compliment. Once a week something they'd never said before on the theme, "I like you because—."

Do you realize what this means, Heather? From my standpoint it means I know hundreds of things my wife likes about me. It also means that I'm hopelessly hooked on her accolades. And this you can bet on too, I'd rather talk my life over with her than any person I know. The trivia. The deep stuff. All of it.

As I've told you, it wasn't always like this with us. There were times when we seemed to be calling across a chasm, "Anybody listening? Anyone over there?"

You know what I mean, don't you? The silence is wide and deep between you and your man. And I'm sorry.

I hope one day Roger will open up to begin closing these

gaps between you. But here's one place where *you* can start. Every day tell him something you like about him. Every week, a fresh compliment. Try it for three months. Six. Two years.

We know one couple who can tell you for sure that "I like you because" is great for openers.

Send Him Out Smiling in the Morning

Dear Heather,

There is considerable difference between a "sight" and a "vision." And which you are early in the morning may count more than you know.

Why do I think of Martha so often during my day? Why do I flash back to her if an attractive woman smiles at me? Why the recall of her nice arrangement of molecules when I see an attractive figure?

Most wives would be glad if their husbands were asking those questions.

So I asked her, "What makes some women a magnet drawing their husbands' thoughts?"

She said it was a lot of little things. And one she mentioned was this, "I think a woman should be easy on the eyes when her husband leaves home in the morning."

I've been pondering that, and looking back I can see it clearly. This "easy-to-remember woman of mine" for years

27

has been working at it. She's been getting up fifteen minutes early to brush her hair and brighten her face. To dress in something attractive for our goodbyes. For years she's organized the children's breakfast the night before so she could concentrate on me. That's what she told me and then she added, "With all those attractive women around, I want to make it easy for you to remember me."

He's a fortunate husband whose wife lights the fires of his imagination every morning.

Men are like this, Heather. If they've got any maleness about them at all, they're going to be thinking of women. You've done a great thing when you keep Roger focusing most of his thoughts on one woman. You.

The cocktail lounges of our land are filled with men who would rather be there than home. But now and then I meet a man like me. He'd rather be home than any place else on earth. He looks forward to seeing his wife again. He wants to hear her voice. To tell her about his day and hear about hers. All day long he's been convincing himself that this is the place, the time, the person.

That's why you do a fine thing when you send him out smiling in the morning.

P.S. I am reminded of a paper I once heard at a symposium. This psychiatrist was reporting on: "Discord in Marital Relationship as a Contributing Factor in Automobile Accidents." Might be another good reason to send him out smiling in the morning.

Francine Sleeps Till 9:00 A.M.

Dear Heather,

Francine sleeps till 9:00 A.M. Wonderful, wonderful sleep. Ernie kisses her goodbye at 7:00. Sometimes she doesn't know it. But if she does, she burrows down for two more hours. (No children.)

Ernie is a computer expert. Well up in management. It's a heavy morning coming up for him every morning.

One day some months ago Francine was shaken up. It was the day of her bridge club, and the members were discussing wifely responsibilities. The subject turned to what the good wife will and won't do early in the morning. The importance of looking nice, feeling nice, sounding nice. Happy thoughts in the early hours for happier husbands all day long. Naturally, Francine thought of herself fast asleep.

Poor Ernie facing the world each day alone.

So Francine decided to mend her ways. She would rise

early from now on. She would cook him a big breakfast. She would be the perfect wife.

Could you guess what happened?

One day recently Ernie announced, "Let's face it, Francine. I like it better when you sleep. I've gained five pounds in thirty days. And I really don't enjoy breakfast. A cup of coffee is all I want. I like to read the paper and think about my day. Besides, I enjoy sitting there remembering how nice you were last night."

I thought you should hear that story. It has an important message. And the message is that every couple should do their own thing.

With all I'm telling you, I hope you'll remember: Just because it's good for 80 per cent, or 90, for one couple or a million, doesn't mean it will do for you.

So long as you know you're getting through to each other, don't you worry about what "they" say.

"A *Time to Keep Silence*"

Dear Heather,

In the Book of Ecclesiastes there is a lovely passage which begins, "To everything there is a season." Then it lists all the interesting things we can do with our time. And I think one of the nicest is this—"There is a time to keep silence."

There is.

In some of our letters, I've told you how we set aside specific time for visiting. Time to court. To have fun. Time for deep sharing of what's going on inside.

Today I want to tell you a little thing I remember about a particular time in my life. It was a period when I was harassed and harried. I was buried under responsibility eight hours a day. Some times it was ten to fifteen hours. Frankly, some days I thought the job was over my head. Some days I knew it was. All the time dozens of people were pressing in on me. Committee meetings. Appointments. Drop-ins. Phone calls. Details. Details.

Now I'm a man who goes strong for the family waiting to welcome Daddy. I love them sitting there on the steps and running down the walk to throw their arms around me. Big hugs from little children and a warm hug from a warm woman, you can't beat it. This is, was, and always will be one of the big reasons men hurry home from work.

But then the time may come in a fellow's career when he will think of his home as a hiding place. A place of retreat from the world.

I don't know when this might be for Roger. I think it depends on the man. But I know it requires a woman's supersensitivity.

I also know that men should be supersensitive to women's special needs. They have their times too. They get buried under the load. But our theme here is how to get your husband to communicate. And one way to get him communicating may be providing him some time pockets for absolute quiet.

I remember vividly the night Martha made this announcement:

From now on, when Daddy comes home we're going to give him fifteen minutes for unwinding. Then will come dinner and a big visit. That's when we'll tell all the fun things and have our good time together.

Some nights I didn't feel like this re-entry period. I wanted to laugh or shoot baskets with the boys. Maybe what I needed then was to sit on the love seat with her and visit. So? That was *my* choice.

Maybe some re-entry time at your house would be worth a try for both you and Roger. A man might talk more to the woman who respects his right not to talk when he doesn't feel like talking.

What Was Your Happiest Moment Today?

Dear Heather,

Sometimes little keys turn big doors. And here's one of those little keys in our marriage.

At night or during the evening (not every night or every evening, but often enough) one of us will ask the question:

"What was your happiest moment today?"

Bedtime. Maybe dinner. Could be when we're out for a walk or sitting together in the living room, one of us asks it.

You sense at once what this does for us. We begin sorting out all the nice things to get to *the* special one for that day.

We know a thing like this might not do for everyone. But if it won't do for you, we hope you'll find something like it.

A famous doctor spent his career studying life's healthiest emotions. At the conclusion of his lifetime research, he said, "There is one attitude which does more to keep you well than any other. It is thanksgiving. Gratitude seems to stimulate the life force and keep it flowing more than any other feeling."

That, says the doctor, is what thanksgiving does for the body. It also does great things for a mind. We have found that it does the same for two bodies and two minds together.

There are couples who need nothing so bad as a computer in their love to file away the good stuff. For reviewing later. For sharing. For healing. For turning on to each other like beautiful.

The Forty-eight-Hour Pledge

Dear Heather,

In this letter let's do a complete switch from the good stuff. We've discussed compliments. Now what can we do with things we don't like?

One of the most effective agreements Martha and I ever made is what we call our "forty-eight-hour pledge."

This consists of a simple promise. It is our compact that we will not hide serious negative feelings for more than forty-eight hours.

A favorite marital quote is the Apostle Paul's "Let not the sun go down on your wrath." This is often used as an admonishment to speed in settling disagreements. Every little problem should be solved before those two heads hit the pillow.

The main thing wrong here is that it's terrible advice. Chances are the Apostle wasn't married.

Sometimes it takes all the strength we have just to go on breathing. We may not be ready to "tell it like it is."

Perhaps our mate isn't up to receiving any hostility right now.

All this requires delicate timing so we can ask for an extension—"I'd like another forty-eight hours to hate you." Which request is usually granted in good humor. Or if it can't be, then the basis is laid for settlement. Great marriages are not all moonlight and roses. In the greatest relationships they have learned to do battle intelligently.

Some agreement for surfacing hostility is ultra important because of the way we're made. There are crucial strata in us from which hostility can be lifted out of consciousness for sharing. But if allowed to remain too long, it will slip into the subconscious and be forgotten. Only it doesn't forget us. Why does he blow up? Because you forgot to get his blue slacks cleaned? Maybe it was because you unintentionally slighted him three weeks ago. You hurt him then, and he didn't tell you. So he's not even aware this is still bugging him.

Unshared resentment creates a subtle emotional smog in the atmosphere of any home. Sharing "the not so nice" in a nice way is an art to be learned. But a smart wife can learn it and teach it to her husband nicely.

Here's another fine thing we did for our communication. It is a deal we agreed to for surfacing our differences. We call this "Our Seven Official Rules for a Good Clean Fight."*

* Detailed explanation of these rules is found in *Letters to Philip,* Doubleday (copyright © 1968 by Charlie W. Shedd and The Abundance Foundation), from a chapter entitled "Fight the Good Fight."

1. BEFORE WE BEGIN WE MUST BOTH AGREE THAT THE TIME IS RIGHT. Sometimes what any good love needs is a war, provided you keep in mind rule #2.

2. WE WILL REMEMBER THAT OUR ONLY AIM IS DEEPER UNDERSTANDING. When some brickbat hits, our normal reaction is to look for something we can throw back. Mature love reacts in a different way. It says, "He's got a problem. How can I help him?"

3. WE WILL CHECK OUR WEAPONS OFTEN TO BE SURE THEY'RE NOT DEADLY. War tacticians use the interesting term "overkill." What they are warning against is slaughtering more than necessary to win. That sounds an important note for conflict in marriage. The wise couple remembers they're not fighting to obliterate each other. They hold the battle line to just the right intensity. If you learn to do this with skill, the heat you generate may warm your marriage later to a very nice temperature.

4. WE WILL LOWER OUR VOICES ONE NOTCH INSTEAD OF RAISING THEM TWO. Obviously, this calls for considerable discipline, but pulverizing each other with words is never good. You can stick to the neuter nouns and sterile adjectives. You can also develop several phrases which can be interpreted different ways. It's a human tendency to make the sound go higher with the mounting ire. But you do a good thing when you agree to say it softly as you say it thoroughly.

5. WE WILL NEVER QUARREL OR REVEAL PRIVATE MATTERS IN PUBLIC. I'll take you over this road again, but right here, note: "When you're quarreling, stay away from

your main source of sympathy outside your home." Your best friend or your mother may sometimes build up your ego to your detriment. Remember, you've finally got to settle it with Roger. You could be wasting valuable time trying to settle it elsewhere.

6. WE WILL DISCUSS AN ARMISTICE WHENEVER EITHER OF US CALLS "HALT." One couple we know invented a clever thing. They have what they call "the committee." This is not some outside influence. It is rather a prearranged signal between them. When one of them says, "I move we refer it to the committee," this means they're ready for cease fire.

7. WHEN WE HAVE COME TO TERMS, WE WILL PUT THE PROBLEM AWAY UNTIL WE BOTH AGREE IT NEEDS MORE DISCUSSING. A great husband-wife relationship does not mean that these two have reached the peak of human coalescing. It more likely indicates they are living up to their capacity for "oneness" today. They know tomorrow will give them more capacity for more total togetherness.

Points to remember:

We will not force more unanimity than our marriage is prepared to handle.

The movement to get things settled is always more important than who started it.

The more enmity you move out, the more room you have for more friendship moving in.

She Gives It to Me Straight

Dear Heather,

I once asked a group of men to write down their thoughts on why they talk. Why they clam up. Who they talk to. Who they wouldn't open up with.

One man wrote a report I thought worth remembering. It's surprising in a way, but maybe it offers some help with particular types.

One reason I talk to my wife is that she always gives it to me straight. Tells me when I'm not thinking right. You know, the whole truth. She lets me have my say and builds up my ego a while. But then when I've said enough, she'll level with me. Always starts the same way, "O.K., Buster." And I know I'm going to get it now. Right between the eyes. She tells me where I could have been wrong, where I need to grow up, or what I might do to straighten it out. Not many guys have wives like that.

He's right. Not many do. Some couples go through life singing nothing but sympathy songs. These add a nice touch when limited. But when they're overdone too long, they make the music mute.

You give Roger too much "Poor Roger." . . . "They aren't being fair to you." . . . "They're wrong, you're right." . . . "The world simply isn't doing what it should by you, dear." . . . plus anything else which keeps him away from the mirror—you keep on giving him this and he'll eventually lose respect for you. Why? Because it's only the truth which sets men free. Only the truth can open roads for total communication.

I'm thinking of Fred who spent the last twenty years of his life at the same dull job. I'm thinking of Gordon who started like an ascending star, but sputtered out to a near blah. I'm thinking of Percy, Harrison, Richard, and a great big baby named Ludwig. These and many more like them went from something to nothing on too much sympathy.

You will sense that leveling with a man is delicate business, an art to be learned. It's really a matter of timing. Experimenting. Testing. Gradually you will discover "how far," "how much" and "when."

Men are a species of complex emotions and needs. Sure, women are that way too. You know more than I do about women's needs. But I know this about ours—we want to be cuddled and coddled sometimes. "Lay it on me soft and soothing, baby." But when the "goo" gets too "gooey," we'll thank you for another thing, STRAIGHT TALK.

Nag Is a Dirty Word

Dear Heather,

All the dirty words in man talk aren't four letters. Any way you spell it, nagging gives off "bad vibes" to the male. Maybe it's because he had too much of this as a child. Even if his mother was one of the gentle women, he got it from somewhere. The family shrew, whoever she was, sounded like the tap, tap, tap of some female hammer. And you can know this for sure, my lonesome friend—Roger's recall for that sound is not far below the surface.

If a woman persists in her nagging, her man will retreat into his own world. He will barricade himself. At first he'll hear you. But when he gets too much, you've had it. The Lord created men with a trap door in each ear as a defense against brawling women.

So what are the alternatives?

One is to be a good sport about some things. Kristy is a classic example of what I have in mind here. She's a supersentimental somebody. She was raised with affection all over the place. But Bruce is a clod when it comes to the little extras, like remembering anniversaries. When they

43

were first married, Kristy took all this personally. She thought if he loved her enough, Bruce would care enough to remember a few things. You know, cologne, candy, "say it with flowers" now and then. But that's not Bruce. He wasn't raised that way.

So Kristy decided to quit nagging. From now on she would announce, "Tuesday's our anniversary, honey, and you're taking me out for dinner." Then she makes the reservations, buys herself a corsage, dresses up in her best, and off they go for their celebration. It really is *their* celebration, because Bruce likes it this way. He thinks that's how they do it in any well-run marriage.

I wish I could tell you she's brought him around. It would be nice to report that he remembers now after seventeen years. But he doesn't, he hasn't, he never will. So Kristy does that for him. And he appreciates it. Some women might feel put upon staging it like this. Not Kristy. She appreciates Bruce for all the good things about him. And she accepts the things that will never change.

Theirs is a fine marriage. In fact I'd give it an "A" when it comes to communicating. She talks. He talks. And if you could see them with each other, you'd know there's a lot of togetherness going on here.

I wouldn't suggest that you demean yourself ever. But I think it's a good idea to put your head to some of these questions:

Is there any place where I have forced Roger to wall himself off in self-defense against my nagging?

Where could I accept the inevitable and make life more fun for both of us?

Mutual Self-Analysis

Dear Heather,

Let's take another look at your statement, "Roger wouldn't be caught dead in a counselor's office. In fact, he won't even go to our minister with me. So what are we going to do?"

Not one thing you can do if Roger continues to stonewall himself. But if he won't get help outside your marriage, there is another possibility. We call it "Mutual Self-Analysis" and it was one of the great forward thrusts in our marriage.

Sure, we know the term "Mutual Self-Analysis" reaches around to cancel itself. "Self" is an individual thing, and "mutual" takes two. But by this method two indivduals can psych themselves out. Then they can share their findings to help each other.

If you need a psychiatrist, run, don't walk to the nearest phone. But if you're only a little flaky like most of us, this could be a terrific thing for both of you.

45

Incidentally, here's a warning (maybe not so incidental either). How you start this could be crucial, and it never works to say, "Roger, you seem to have a problem. Let us now approach it."

So you're telling me this *is* Roger's problem. Let's say that's true. It's still your problem together, isn't it? Can't you say, "Roger, *we* have a problem"? On this basis you're not calling him to the judgment seat. You're calling him to sit down with you and work it out together. Whatever is hard for you to say, you'll say. Where you need help, you'll admit it. You'll let it all hang out. Absolute honesty is an absolute must.

But the fascinating things you'll find to share with each other will more than make up for the toughies.

When you once get started with all this, you're headed for some great discoveries. There is no journey in the world so exciting as the journey inside you.

I Corinthians 13 has been called the most beautiful combination of words ever written on love. You will note that the only phrase repeated in that chapter is "We know in part."

That is a wonderful fact for which we can thank our Creator. He made us this way. So there are vast ranges of undiscovered terrain waiting for those who begin this trip together. No couple, going at it right, could ever possibly exhaust the faraway places. This is like climbing mountains. You make it to the top of one, and you see more to be explored in the distance.

We can tell you this goes on at least thirty-five years. And we fully expect that it goes on forever and forever. That is some kind of exciting, isn't it?

To do it the way we do it calls for a definite time commitment. We have agreed to spend fifteen minutes a day at this. Fifteen minutes to talk about what's going on inside Charlie and Martha. Sometimes it's mostly monologue, depending on who's hurting. Then again it could be a rapid exchange or a slow dredging up of some ancient fear. Often we go beyond the prescribed time. Many of our happiest memories have come from these moments.

Reading is another important part of our mutual self-analysis. Sometimes we read together and discuss. More likely we've been studying the same book at different times. While we read, we mark things to be shared. You wouldn't believe the scribbles in our books. An arrow for some section which pins us to the wall. A candle for new insights. One, two, three stars for more important sections. And sometimes if the author paints us into a corner, we mark "me." (I never put "Martha" and she never writes "Charlie.") Mutual self-analysis requires mutual respect.

On this basis, then, we come to our daily visit. Now we can check the places where we've found ourselves. We can ask and receive honest answers. "Am I *really* like this? Could *that* be why I do these crazy things?"

There is no way I could describe what this has done for us. Release from nervous tension. Permanent burial of certain old fears. Memories healed. Some fissure has closed. A hurt has been laid away. Order restored inside. It happens like a flash, or without our knowing it. Then again, it may come slowly over a long period of time. We share, and six weeks later something in us feels better.

Echoes of the Quaker saying: "I felt the evil in me weakened and the good raised up."

No matter your method, the name of the game is *talk*. Talk regularly. Talk totally. Communication has to start somewhere. So if you think you're mature enough, why not invite Roger to a mutual experiment? A fascinating experiment just for the two of you?

Ask him to agree on fifteen minutes a day. Seems like such a little deal, doesn't it? But it could become one of the biggest deals ever for your marriage. It could make all the difference between a lonesome road and a beautiful friendship.

Mercy

Dear Heather,

The story you are about to hear is true. I tell you this, because it sounds far out.

Once upon a time there was a very shy young thing. She was shy because some people are shy. She was also shy because she'd been brought up that way. She was shy because no man had ever told her she was beautiful, which she was.

Then the shy girl married an outgoing "patter of backs." He was a phony in one sense. He kept going out to keep from going in. Some people do chatter incessantly so they won't hear the inner voices. They even make other people laugh to keep from facing the truth about themselves.

That's how he was. Can you imagine a shy girl married to such a character? You know there would be conflict. Plus a heavy load of jealousy. So much conflict and jealousy they were both miserable. Sure, they had some good times, but always in the shadows, this question: What if "hail-fellow-well-met" was overly attractive to other women? Some women are so lonely they can't tell a faker from the real thing. What if??? Just suppose???

Now that would be some monster for a shy girl to wrestle, wouldn't it? But she wrestled it and won. And he'll never forget that day she made her announcement. She sat him down and said, "I have made friends with this awful thing inside me. We have quarreled about it for the last time. How I have made friends with it is that I have decided nothing, absolutely nothing is ever going to break us up. If you *should* have an affair, come home and tell me. Of course, I will be hurt, but I will listen and I will not be angry. We will discuss it. And even while it is going on, will you remember that I'm loving you?"

Did you ever hear of a better way to ruin a man's fun? No one in his right mind would play loose with a love like that. And you can guess how I know that in thirty-five years he's never been unfaithful. You will also sense that his loyalty to her is not because he's good, but because she is.

Psychologists are right. No person will ever reveal himself unless he's assured that what he offers will be received with mercy. That makes sense, doesn't it? If I show you all of me and you don't like it, I have nothing left. But if I know you'll like me anyway, then I have nothing to fear.

Well, maybe your marriage isn't ready for this. Some women couldn't do it and mean it. But what a great goal!

And you can start being kind right now. When a man is sure his wife won't be judgmental, he can begin surfacing himself. He can risk coming out from behind his façades a bit. And when he finds she means it, he can reveal more and more.

Everyone in the world has a dream of one day opening up completely. Some never find the place nor the person where that dream can come true.

Somehow you must let Roger know you are the place, you're the person. With you he can be the real Roger unafraid.

When he knows that for sure, you've taken a major step toward great friendship.

Lust or Appreciation

Dear Heather,

If you could read all the sexy sex in a man's mind, you'd probably be scared silly. And you might even decide to stay confined in your own quarters.

Fact is, the average man thinks about sex a lot more than most women know. Men also think about sex much more than most women think about sex. I've told you some places I think men are a collapse. Here's one place the average male deserves a medal—that the rape statistics are no higher than they are. I think it speaks well for masculine control.

The greatest male-female relationship I know has a fine thing going here. This couple lives on a beach where women swim in bikinis and stroll in bikinis. They also loll in bikinis.

Some men are leg men. Some have a thing for the beautiful bosom. Some are especially appreciative of a well-rounded derriere. This particular man I'm telling you about likes all women and almost all of each woman. His wife knows that's true. So she gets him talking, comparing, and they make a wonderful game of it.

She tells him, "We'll say it's never a sin so long as you can tell me what you're thinking."

So fine to live with a woman like that. She's a cleansing force, a purifier.

You do a great thing for the communication between you when you get this message through. "I invite you to communicate what other men must hide. In every way we will enjoy your maleness together."

I can't imagine any man who wouldn't be grateful for a woman like this. She has helped him change lust to appreciation for all women and for her.

With a woman like that, a man doesn't need to go prowling. He has everything he needs here, including a place to talk.

Apology

Dear Heather,

"Love is never having to say you're sorry."

Don't you believe it. It's a widely quoted line from a best seller. It's also been heard by millions who saw the movie.

But there's one outstanding thing wrong with it. It isn't true.

Sure, there are some lovers who might buy it. But the great ones know something else. Not far behind the three little words "I love you" are four more, "I'm sorry. Forgive me."

Some men simply can't apologize or won't. Roger may be one of these, but if he is, it probably isn't your fault. Something happened long before he met you to cauterize his apologizer. I know many women who have agonized a long time with such characters, and some forever.

But there are at least two things you might keep in mind. One is you can tell him you're sorry even if it is mostly his fault. Another is that you can give him a chance to express his regrets even if he can't say them.

That's what Ruth did.

Mike is a traveling salesman. Very much a man, but very much hung up some ways. Because he couldn't unbend enough to express his regret, she did an interesting thing. One week when he took off on Monday, she wrote him a note. She packed it in his bag where he'd be sure to find it. She told him how much she cared about their relationship. She was sorry for whatever she'd done wrong. Would he please forgive her for any part she played in their problem right now? (She told me, not him, she couldn't even think of one place where she was at fault in this particular fracas.) Then she wished him a good trip and told him she'd be praying for him and for them.

If a man found a note like this and still couldn't apologize, what would he do? He might do what Mike did. He stopped at the florist and bought her a dozen red roses. No, he's still never said, "I'm sorry. Forgive me." But she got the message.

Ruth is a wise woman. She did two things any wise woman can do with any fuss under any circumstance. She let him know she was sorry things weren't going well between them. And she gave him a chance to say the same thing his way.

If a man ever did feel like talking, he'd know one thing for sure. A woman like Ruth might be one fine place to begin.

How Not to Keep Him Talking

Dear Heather,

Some things I can't tell you, because I've never been a woman. No matter what the unisexers say, there *are* gender differences. For which any real man would praise the Lord.

So it makes sense that I know some things you don't. And what I know is that a man will clam up every time with a certain type wife.

I'm going to give you here a list for starters. These are women I know. You can probably add some people you know.

Examples of how not to keep him talking:

1. *She constantly compares him to the more successful.*
"Did you know the Andersons are moving into their new home this week? I understand it's simply elegant. Must be nice!"
So?

How long has it been since you told your man how proud you are of what he's doing?

2. *She snipes at things he can never change.*
"Doesn't Sidney Jones have the most beautiful wavy hair?"

So?

Doesn't any balding husband know he's getting balder by the year?

3. *She tells him how he should have done it.*
"I just knew you should have fired that woman long ago. But you wouldn't listen."

So?

There isn't a man alive who responds favorably to a continual barrage of "I told you so."

4. *She constantly puts him down for what he can't do naturally.*
"If anything gets fixed around here, I have to do it."

So?

You can use the telephone, can't you? How about a word of gratitude that he earns enough for you to pay the repairman?

5. *She compares his family unfavorably with hers.*
"My grandfather was a preacher and two of my uncles were."

So?

By the time they got to you, what happened to all that holiness?

6. *She is forever dredging up old boy friends.*

"Wasn't that a beautiful tenor solo this morning? He sang so much like Wendell Watson."

So?

Doesn't he know you gave Wendell up because all he could do was sing? If you wanted a canary, why didn't you say so?

7. *She throws the garbage in his face the minute he gets home.*

"The broken hinge on the back door screen. . . . Scratch on the right front fender. . . . Plumber can't come till Thursday. . . . Junior got another failing slip, et cetera ad nauseum."

So?

How about making a list of the good things too? It would be better for you and him. You can give the bad news slow and gradual.

We could go on a long time, but this stuff is a drag, isn't it? However, there *is* one more turn-off I want you to think about long and hard. I've had enough of this for today and I imagine you have. So let's cut it off right here and save the heavy for our next letter.

I Will Never Tell Gladys Again

Dear Heather,

We've talked about not putting Roger down when he can hear you do it. That's bad. But when you put him down and he *isn't* around, that could be even worse.

Then there's one more thing which can be deadly. This is telling something you should have kept secret. There are several ways these confidential items might get back to a man. Somebody overheard you. Or somebody you told it to in secret might drop it into their conversational stream. They didn't mean to, you know. Did it without thinking. Maybe they even have a subconscious thing going which makes them allergic to secrets.

I have a feeling you can't get by with this. Something in the universe works against the woman whose tongue hangs in the middle and wags at both ends. This gal is asking for real trouble. One day her remarks come back to the vicinity where they started.

Here's a vivid example of what I mean. I happen to be

working with this couple now, so it's fresh in my mind. When they first came to me, he started with:

"I will never again tell Gladys anything confidential. Never! Ever!"

That's what he told me, and I hope he's only over-reacting.

What happened in this case I must keep secret. So all I need to tell you is that after Fred told Gladys, she told her best friend. Her best friend told her husband. Her husband accidentally dropped the story one day at the club. Of all places, it was in the men's room. And would you believe, unseen on the john sat the one guy who never should have heard it. The boss. Next day Fred was called on the carpet and they worked him over, but good.

That's why he says, "I will never again tell Gladys anything confidential. Never! Ever!"

You can bet she's sorry. She's told him so a dozen times, or three dozen. You can also bet she means it and I hope one day he'll believe her. But some things a man remembers long. And this is one of the hardest for him to forget—that the woman he'd like to talk with can't really be trusted.

About the only good thing to be said for their story is that it could be worse. As in this knotty little scenario from the life of Gloria and Norman.

One day at bridge she kiddingly made a remark reflecting on Norman's manliness. It really was a side-splitter and it did fit in with the conversation. In fact, it was so funny some of the girls took it home to their husbands. They thought it was uproarious too.

That's why one of the guys told it at the office coffee break on Monday.

You guessed it.

Somebody carried it back to Norman. Of course, it had been exaggerated. Considerably. It was all out of proportion by now and Norman simply couldn't believe it. Would Gloria really say a thing like that?

She's a loving person, Gloria. Kind. And when she heard it back, she couldn't believe it either the way it had grown. So she could understand how much it hurt Norman. She apologized and told him exactly what she'd said. Then when he heard it the way she'd told it, he could understand it better. It really was funny that way. But back somewhere in his mind there is that sneaking question: Why did she ever say it in the first place?

The reason I know is that they've been coming to me for several sessions now. We're working hard to put it where it belongs and I think we'll make it.

But write this on your heart for sure, Heather—some things should never go beyond your front door!

There is an ugly variation of all this which any smart couple will guard against. That's the nasty little spectacle of putting each other down in public. I mean out loud and right out there in the open.

This is a quirk in some marriages. It says some things about couples who have the bad manners to do it. Obviously, they're not surfacing their hostility in the right place, behind their own closed doors.

Some psychologists say these people wait till they have

an audience for another reason. They lack the courage to confront each other in private. They feel more secure in public. If the whole thing becomes a donnybrook here, someone might come to their rescue. But whatever the reason, don't do it. It's not very couth and it's never a positive for communication.

Now let's close on a winner.

We once knew a prominent public figure who taught us a great thing. Fortunately, it was early in our marriage. He was an elected official who campaigned every four years. Good speaker. Fine man. And very much in love with his wife.

Because of our relationship, I've heard him talk many times. And every time he'd close the same way. It affected me deeply, so I can give you his ending, word for word.

"When you've been in politics as long as I have, folks, you can bet you get cussed and discussed. You make a lot of friends and some otherwise. You gain a lot of votes and lose some. But I want you all to know that if they ever come and tell me, 'John, you got two votes,' I'll know who voted for me besides myself." Then, turning to his wife he would say, "Mama, you come on up here. I want these folks to meet the best darn press agent any man ever had."

The first time Martha and I heard him say that, we took the pledge. We committed ourselves permanently to an impregnable loyalty outside our home.

And you can count on this, Heather. Your man doesn't need to be a politician to appreciate a woman like that.

Money

Dear Heather,

Mrs. McCloud didn't know thing one about her husband's business. He thought she shouldn't be bothered. McCloud men had always handled the family finances. They had been trained like that and he believed it was the only way.

He provided well for her. Gave her a handsome allowance. She didn't want for one thing. Which was all just great for Mrs. McCloud so long as Mr. McCloud was there to keep it going.

But today he's in a nursing home. Can't talk. Can't write. All he can do is move his head for "yes" and "no." And that's tough because his mind is apparently unaffected. Their children live far away. She's making out with the help of a good lawyer, but sometimes I ask myself: Does Mr. McCloud wonder now if he did right to keep her so uninstructed?

I've known others like the McClouds with certain blind spots in their communication. That's why it always makes me nervous when a woman says, "Money is one thing we don't talk about."

There is a special reason why I wanted to write you this letter. I know one marriage where the wife refused to be kept in the dark. When they started their life together, her husband managed the books. He'd never had much, so now at the end of their schooling this was a big deal for him. A bit of an ego trip for his maleness.

At first his wife, being very wise, let him get by with it. Then one day she confronted him eyeball to eyeball. "The time has come," she announced, "for me to know what's coming in and going out." She gave him her reasons, including all the long-range possibilities. She kept at it nicely until she made a believer out of him. At last he saw the light and that was one of the first places they began communicating. It also proved to be one of the most interesting things they did together. Out of that early communication, they developed a formula on which they agreed:

Give 10 per cent.

Save 10 per cent.

And spend the rest with thanksgiving and praise. From this agreement has grown one of the most exciting aspects of their marriage today. That's why I say you have a right to force Roger's hand where you have rights. Unless he's out of his mind, he'll get the message.

Some things about money a woman does need to know.

It's Too Late Now

Dear Heather,

Today's letter will have a somber tone. I'm about to tell you a sad story. A true story of a woman who put her children ahead of her husband. I know all the facts, because I've been hoping to salvage this marriage. But to put it in technical language, the prognosis is somewhat guarded. Which means it could go either way. She'd like to repair the damage, but he's more than a little skeptical. He's been lonesome so many years, it's hard to believe they could make it.

He doesn't want a divorce really. He just wants it to go on the way it is forever. A divorce would hurt him at the company. He's one of the owners. It would also cost so much to split things down the middle and keep two households going. Then it would mean embarrassment with their friends. Not many of them know what's going on. There would also be talk at the church and the club. That would be unfortunate. At the church he's on the board now, and she's president of the women. At the club they both play golf and have so many contacts.

These last two years he's been especially lonesome. Reason? His wife had literally latched onto their youngest daughter. She's one of those hang-on-to-your-children-for-dear-life mothers. She took it very hard when each of them left for college. But this year when the last one enrolled at the university, she came unglued. Suddenly the house seemed so empty. So big.

Now the lady is turning to her husband, hoping. She's making sounds. Gestures. With all of her womanly wiles, she's letting him know she'd like to be friends again. With a part of himself, he'd like that too, but he's having an awesome struggle.

When was the last time they were close? Was it when they were going together? Or maybe before the first baby came? He simply can't remember and he can't forget the bitterness.

All those years in second place he'd made a life of his own. Had to. Shared things with the fellows he'd rather have shared with her. Yes, he even found other feminine ears for a certain kind of talk. Not right. Of course it isn't. But a man wants a woman with that all-important exchange factor in their communication. All these years his wife has been talking to him, at him, seldom with him.

Lonely is sad at any age. But somehow this one gets me. Think of the fun they could be having now if they had developed a friendship.

Heather, bend your ear down here.

I know too many men who, when their children came, turned down a lonesome road. And when you've gone too long single file, it's hard coming back to double. So much has happened alone it just seems easier to say, "It's too late now."

You're wise to be caring so early. Plus, you're wise to keep checking priorities.

You *can* be both mother and wife. But the wise woman remembers she will begin *and* end as a wife.

Learn His Interests

Dear Heather,

Arthur is a stock market analyst straight from Dullsville. He can talk forever about dividends, prime notes, profits and loss. But when it comes to relating away from the brokerage, he's a total collapse.

If I read the signals right, their name is legion. Thousands of men like him. Plus thousands of lonesome wives struggling to live with these characters.

Patty is one of the strugglers, but failure is not her thing. For several years she's been putting aside a little from her household allowance. She attends investment seminars and is a member of a stocks and bonds study group. She's bought a little of this, a little of that. Lost some, picked a few winners. Then when she had enough confidence, she leveled with Arthur. And here's what she says:

"It's an amazing thing. I know he gained a new respect

71

for me. And he even asks my advice sometimes. He seems to feel I represent the non-professional viewpoint he needs. Now and then he slips in a little talk on other subjects. I actually think maybe we're going to make it after all."

So here's a tip of the hat to all smart women who live by the old adage, "If you can't lick them, join them."

A lot of men have one-track minds. But some of these can be diverted on to the side tracks of more meaningful communication.

Same song, next verse: Most progress in marriage comes slowly. But if you care enough about your husband, here's one more thing you can do. Learn whatever expertise you can in his field.

It may be a fine investment.

Let's Hear It for Enid

Dear Heather,

Only time for a quickie today. So I thought you might like this one about Enid.

Sounds like a character out of some English novel. Looks like it too. Prim. Proper. But really warm under all that dignity. And she couldn't care less about football. Unfortunately for her, Si is practically mesmerized by the stuff from September to New Year's Day.

She gave it a good try. Went to games. Watched games. Even read a boring book or two. But alas, football wasn't her thing. She still doesn't know a punt from a linebacker. But she's crazy about Si. And he is about her. Why not? Here is a quote from one of her letters:

Several years ago I came to the conclusion he'd never change. So I've changed my attitude. Now during the games I pull up my chair beside him and do my needlepoint. At the commercials we visit. And I serve us a snack between halves. I never thought I'd live to say it, but I actually look forward to football season. I can tell this is a new dimension for him too, our being together in a very special way.

But this is what I wanted to say. Since I quit complaining about football, things have been better for us in every way. During the other eight months he actually makes an effort to talk about things I enjoy.

So let's hear it for Enid.

And for any woman who takes her man's obsession and turns it into fun.

. . . and Sarah Beth

Dear Heather,

We live on an island where people come to play golf. They come to golf weekends. To golf on vacation. They come for summer golf and winter golf. And some of them retire here for full-time golf.

Retirement can be a lonesome time, particularly if a couple hasn't communicated through the years. Now they simply have more time not to communicate.

But Sarah Beth wouldn't sit still for this. What she did has a lot to say. Hugh was a successful salesman, who, when he wasn't gone selling, was gone on golf. For several years they vacationed here before their permanent move. Hugh would drop her at the motel and head for the clubhouse. Good thing she liked the beach.

But one bright sunny afternoon, as she was pondering their future, this whole ridiculous deal fell in on her. Two years from now he'd retire. And then what? Then they'd move here, and she'd be a golf widow 100 per cent of the time.

So she made a decision. It's one of the beautiful stories I know on the theme "How to Get Your Husband to Communicate."

Because Hugh traveled a lot, she had a chance to do some things on the sly. And what she did was to take up golf. How could a woman keep that a secret for two years? Well, some men don't give a thought to what their wives do when they're gone. He didn't. So she worked hard. Stayed with her lessons diligently. Kept improving her game. She'll never be a champion. But they're probably out on the course right now having the time of their lives together. With her handicap, she might even beat him today.

Lots of ways to turn a man on, aren't there? If you could hear Hugh tell about Sarah Beth and what she did, you'd love it. I've heard it twenty times or thirty.

But that isn't all. I wish you could see them having dinner in one of our restaurants; at church on Sunday morning; shopping together in our grocery store. I think you'd have the feeling I have. It's worth everything it takes right now toward great communication in the retirement years together.

Hobbies

Dear Heather,

Some couples I know use a mutual hobby to begin communicating.

Chandler is a distinguished professor. He writes erudite papers, lectures on heavy stuff, and spends many hours in the library.

Meta is very much in love with Chandler. She adores him, but she'd be first to tell you she doesn't understand him. She loves to be near him, but what in the world would they talk about?

I'll tell you. Birds.

It started rather casually and then it picked up speed. They bought some bird books, went to bird lectures, took trips. Twenty years later, they are among the best of the bird watchers. This weekend you would probably find them out together looking for rare birds. Or for something new and different. This summer they'll be traveling to some exotic islands.

Meta still doesn't understand the lectures Chandler gives and the courses he's teaching. But she doesn't care, and he doesn't. They can talk about birds.

Vick and Winnie are about to retire. He's only fifty, with fifteen years to go in the company. Has a good job which he enjoys most of the time. But what he really enjoys all the time is the hobby they share.

Vick is a happy woodworker. Loves his shop. Crazy about tools. Feels so fine when he's covered with sawdust, shuffling around in the shavings.

Winnie has always been big on decoupage and painting. She knows antiques and how to finish them. Everybody flips for her original wall plaques, ornaments, furniture decorations.

One Christmas several years ago Vick and Winnie made some interesting gifts for friends and relatives. He cut them out and she painted them. They were a smash. Folks bought them up so fast Vick and Winnie decided to go into business.

Here they are at fifty, with more than they can handle as a side line. At the prime of life, they're ready now to go into something new and different.

Sounds like fun, doesn't it? And it is. Plus, it's also one of the finest marriage friendships we know.

Wish you could meet some others we know. Dr. and Mrs. Browning digging up and down the East coast for old glass. Jack and Anna Hansen, experts on camellias. The

Logans collecting coins. And the Millers building organs together.

Hobbies can be a bringer-together like beautiful. Maybe you and Roger could do a little scratching around in your current common interests. You might come up with something fun for both of you. I mean now. And wouldn't it be fine if it led to a real turned-on friendship later?

Nadine Goes Big for Social Service

Dear Heather,

Nadine is a pink lady.

On Tuesday and Thursday she puts on her pink uniform and goes to the hospital. She likes it especially in the children's ward. Also with the new babies. But she takes her turn at the ordinary jobs—the desk, carrying flowers, the library cart, answering phones.

Nadine has two children, both school age. She's a good mother, good housekeeper, good cook. But that isn't all she does.

On Monday, Wednesday, and Friday Nadine goes to school. She always wanted to be a nurse. It'll take her two years, or three. But she'll get there.

Harry is traffic manager at the airport. Interesting job. He studies routes, schedules, makes decisions, meets fascinating people.

If you could talk to Nadine about Harry's job and what she's doing, she would tell you:

Before I started school and began working at the hospital, I must have been a bore to Harry. He had so many exciting things to tell me. I had so little to offer. Sure, I could tell him about the children, but you know, nothing new. Now my days are so full, we always have plenty to talk about. So I think he likes my doing these things. And I'll tell you for sure, I like myself a whole lot better.

That's the way she puts it. And it just goes to prove— Some women do better *in* the home when they spend some time *out* of it.

Good question for any wife. Would I be a more challenging communicator if I were doing more for other people?

Beamed to His Signal

Dear Heather,

We have a friend whose husband is a ham-radio nut. The problem with being married to these characters is not that they won't communicate. In fact, they are communicating all the time. But it's always across town. Across country. Or to the uttermost parts of the earth.

Hannah says there is one good thing about it. She always knows where Harvey is.

And then sometimes you can do a lot with a man by learning his lingo.

Example?

"Harvey, would it interest you to know that my receiver is beamed right now in your direction?"

Hannah says it gets him every time.

Being a man, I would think so!

Libby Visits the Prostitute

Dear Heather,

Libby is the perfect Southern lady. She looks like something out of a movie. You almost expect, when you meet her, to see a plantation in the background. Very beautiful. But also very naïve.

Only Libby decided to do something about her naïveté.

What happened was a big surprise. Suddenly Libby's husband began to taper off some places. Important places, and when she put her mind to this, she decided to check it out. What she found was downright alarming. This man of hers was more than a little interested in his sexy secretary. Good secretary. Shorthand, eighty words per minute. Plus miscellaneous other attributes.

The more Libby thought about this, the more she didn't like it. She'd been giving her very best. Doing what she knew to do, putting herself into it. Whatever could be wrong? The more she pondered, the more she decided to take action.

So Libby hit on a plan, a daring plan. She went to her brother and asked him to make her an appointment.

Are you ready for this?

She asked him to make an appointment for her with his favorite prostitute. He did and she went. She paid the lady for her time and asked some questions. Mostly she asked, "What do you do for a man which I'm not doing? I mean, what do you do to keep him coming back?"

The last time I saw Libby, she came running across an airport lobby.

"Oh, Dr. Shedd, Dr. Shedd," she called, on the wing. She threw her arms around me with this glad exclamation, "It worked, it worked."

Then she capped her exciting story, "He wouldn't have time now, nor energy, for anyone but me. Besides he's having so much fun, and I am. And we're closer than we've ever been before."

So what's the lesson for today?

The lesson is: Body communication the way he likes it may lead to total communication the way you like it.

What the Prostitute Told Libby

Dear Heather,

Whenever I tell Libby's story at seminars and women's meetings, I know this for sure. In the discussion period someone is certain to ask, "What did the prostitute tell Libby?"

Fair question.

Two answers:

First, be aggressive some of the time. Almost every man appreciates a snow job now and then. Even the guys who like to think of themselves as cavemen go for change occasionally.

So here's a question for you. How long has it been since you met Roger at the door and poured on the coals? The woman who always waits is missing an important fact. Her man needs to be needed too.

You've done a wonderful thing when you let him know how important he is here. Sometimes when his ego is down and he's feeling low, what he needs is you, warm and yearning.

And sometimes when his ego is up, he'll like you then, with your thermostats up.

Here's a second thing the prostitute told Libby. "We let the men try anything and everything. What they're afraid to do with their wives, we encourage them to do with us."

I don't think any woman should put up with anything damaging to her emotions. Or physically harmful. But even in this enlightened day, some have never heard the message:

"There is nothing wrong with anything any couple wants to try sexually between them. Provided they both want to try it, and it won't harm either, have fun!"

Some men want certain kinds of sex which come as a surprise to some women. And unless someone clues you in ahead of time, you may think them downright bizarre.

They're really not. Some of these are natural for total expression of the total man. I've heard psychiatrists explain the unusual approaches. And they make good sense. Every man hopes some day he can be totally intimate with a woman. Some of the things which seem odd to us, aren't odd at all in this light. They are the natural working out of life-long repression.

We'll close this letter with a few sentences out of another letter. It's from a young wife who says,

Thank you for telling me all these things about unusual sex. When I came down off my high and mighty, so many things got better between us. And I know you'll understand when I say, I found it all very enjoyable when I changed my attitude.

So have fun, and here's a principle worth remembering—
  The man who can do anything he feels
    like doing with a woman,
  Is more likely to say everything he feels
    like saying.

Are *Some Men Hopeless?*

Dear Heather,

Let's say you've given him the full treatment. You've done all the things smart women do. You've turned up your thermostat and let him know it's getting warm around here.

Same result every time—zero!

Comes now the question: *Are* some men hopeless?

I think the answer is yes, some men are hopeless.

Who?

Those who absolutely refuse to change.

I see these men and their wives often in the consultation room. And here's the list of hopeless husbands in order of their frequency. With each I'm quoting from some suffering woman.

1. *The alcoholic or problem drinker.*

"He's a wonderful person when he's sober. But he's sober so seldom any more. Do you know how desolate life can be with a man who drinks, watches TV, and goes to sleep in his chair? Can you imagine how repulsive it gets to be every night when he finally comes to bed smelling like a brewery. Of course, he turns me off, completely!"

2. *The constantly unfaithful.*

"I can't figure him out. I thought we were happy. From talking with my friends, I think we have it better than most couples. But it seems he has this thing inside which simply must have other women. I can't help taking it as a personal insult. Every time it happens, it seems to destroy a little more of my self-respect."

3. *The money mad, hell-bent for success.*

"He kept using the excuse that we'd really live when he made his first million. So he made it and now he wants more. I've been watching this sinister attitude creep up on the children and I can't let it happen to them. I've just about decided there is nothing I can do, because it's a disease and he can't believe he's sick."

4. *The tyrant. Cruel. Hitler type.*

"Do you know how hard it is to live with a man whose idea of getting along is 'You do it my way and that's co-operation.' If we ever cross him, he bears down that much harder. I think he is trying to get back at all of us for what his parents did to him, and I think he hates women. I've had it."

5. *The impotent.*

"I feel so sorry for him. He seems to be sexually dead. Completely dead. We haven't made love in six months and I'm about to go out of my mind. He's ashamed to talk to a doctor or go to anyone for help. Then he warns me never to mention it. He's forcing me to make a decision I don't want to make."

6. *The insanely jealous.*

"He wakes me up at night sometimes to grill me. Who did I see yesterday? Why did I smile at Russell like that? Who was I talking to on the phone when he came home? He must really know I have never been unfaithful, but I am getting physically exhausted and completely worn out every other way."

7. *The "you-need-a-psychiatrist" projector.*

Thousands and thousands of husbands project their problem with, "If only *you* would change." . . . "If *you* would make a few simple alterations." . . . "If *you'd* get help." . . . "If *you* were different," et cetera ad infinitum. It's all part of the refusal barrage. And so long as he sounds that refrain, he's hopeless.

8, 9, 10, 23, and 116. The list goes on.

Some men lose themselves in causes to keep from being found by anyone. I've heard from lonesome wives whose husbands were compulsive church workers. Compulsive politicians. Compulsive servers of causes too numerous to mention. Compulsive fishermen, hunters, golfers, anything. Each with his different shading, but all with this in common:

The bridge between them and their wives was broken at one end. And the man who isn't willing to repair it, not even a bit from his end, he's hopeless.

I've known women who said, "I married him for better or for worse and I'm staying." Some of these were heroic. I admire them. But others are not at all admirable. They may only be feeling good, because they're feeling bad. Shades of a martyr complex.

I believe you when you say you would go a long way if Roger would only come a short distance. But if he won't, then you and all the others like you are down to two choices:

1. You can take what he gives you and live on the scraps of relationship. You can build a life for yourself around his "aloof."

2. You can check out.

Grim, isn't it? You're choosing from two different kinds of unhappiness. And if you opt for number two, you've come to some very tough questions: What can I do for a living? Where will we go, the children and I? Will I be more lonesome alone than with him? Will there be someone else some day?

That last one could be a whammy! I once heard a psychiatrist on the theme "Divorce Won't Help Neurotics."

He's right. Some people go from failure to failure. Until

they have corrected their character flaws, they'd be better off alone. Psychiatrists call them "symbiotics," problems looking for matching problems. And chances are good they'll find them.

You know some fine second marriages. So do I. But the best preparation for one of these is a long look in the mirror. Where did *you* fail? What did *you* do wrong? How could *you* do better? Do *you* honestly have more to offer now because of your experience?

Until you have faced these questions, another marriage may be nothing more than whistling past the next graveyard. I wish I could give you some assurance. Some absolute guarantees about your future. No way. I've known results both good and bad. Some decided to tough it out and they were sorry. Some decided to tough it out and they were glad. Some severed connections and things went well. Some severed connections and things were awful. I've married some second-time-arounders and they were happy. I've married some and they weren't.

Maybe the fairest thing to say is that there isn't an answer anywhere else but inside you. Only I think it would have to be decided on a basis something like this. When you become so demeaned that your self-respect is jeopardized, you're getting close to the border.

I do think there are times when it is more honorable not to live with someone than to continue the relationship.

And above all, I hope you can stay tuned to the One who has all the answers, and understands.

The Duet of Prayer

Dear Heather,

Today is "Be Nice to Martha Day."

I got up this morning and decided that's what it would be. My wife deserves the best. Think of her first, Charlie. Be extra loving. Do something special for her. Pay her a compliment at breakfast. This is the day to be a perfect husband.

Great idea, isn't it? Noble resolve.

You know how long that lasts? Thirty minutes when I'm at my best. Less than that when I'm not. And some days it's more like thirty seconds.

What's the matter? The matter is I'm human. With me, it simply isn't possible to be unselfish on my own, not for long.

That's how we are, Heather. Husbands come in every size, every style, every shape. But we all have this in common: we're human. And human too much of the time means me first, me second, me third. Then if there's anything left, I'll have that too.

I wish I could report that this serious condition improves as the years go by. But maybe it won't. Some things will never improve without help from the outside.

In our last letter we considered the question, "*Are some men hopeless?*" To which the honest answer must be "Yes" if they refuse to open up. Some doors have latches only on the inside. And that's how the door is to a man's heart. If he absolutely will not turn that latch, any woman married to him is doomed to loneliness. Now she must live on his scraps. If she can't do that, she is faced with some grim options.

That's a brief review of the bad news from our last letter. Now here's the good news. There is still one hope. The Bible says, "With God all things are possible."

That is a fact. I know it's a fact. I know from personal experience that a barricaded man can be opened up through prayer.

Early in our marriage Martha and I decided we'd try an experiment. If we couldn't relate fully on human levels, maybe there was another level worth investigating.

I've told you of several key decisions we made. Agreements. But our biggest agreement ever is right here—

We agreed one day to find out if prayer is for real.

It is.

Not that it was easy. It wasn't. And one of the first difficulties was a language barrier. Most people find it that way and you might. Even if you know how to talk to God alone, it isn't so natural with someone else listening. Praying out loud in another's presence will probably make you nervous at the outset. It will seem as if you're talking a double language.

You'd like to be honest with God, but what would your husband think? Then, if you're honest with him, is that the right language for God? So you're confused. Embarrassed. Tongue-tied. Uncertain.

One day Martha and I decided on a new method. We would begin again. This time we would start praying together in silence. We would discuss ahead of time the things we wanted to pray about. We'd honestly share the concerns of our hearts. We wouldn't argue, wouldn't pass judgment. We would listen and ask questions. Clarify. Then we would pray silently, each of us going to God in his own way. And we'd do this every day. Some times oftener.

For us it is absolutely the greatest and it can be like this for you. If you go at it right and do it regularly, your duet can become a three-way communication.

[THE THIRTY-FIFTH LETTER]

The Happy Surprises of Prayer

Dear Heather,

When I was seven my father gave me a puzzle. I had the mumps right then, and I needed something to occupy my time.

It was a wooden puzzle shaped like a ball. Numerous pieces. Interesting designs. Various sizes.

I knew it wasn't impossible, because it came put together. In its original shape, it was very attractive. But taken apart it was a mess. Challenging. Exciting. But a mess.

For days I worked on it. This way. That way. Every way. And at last I decided there was no way. So I put it in the box, every last piece of it, and called my sister. Would she please take this horrible thing and remove it far, far away. Take it to school. Take it to the trash. Take it anywhere out of my sight forever.

But you know how these things do when you finally call

it quits. They won't quit on you. Next day, there it was in my head again. And my sister, God bless her chubby little intuition, had picked up on that possibility. Instead of discarding it as per instructions, she'd taken it to her room. Nice! Somehow she sensed her chubby brother might go for one more try.

Thank you, Mary Frances! That day, that very day, I discovered the secret. Big surprise. You start at the center, see, and go from there.

Right there at the center, look. These two wooden rings. Slip these over the main peg and everything fits together. Beautiful. Like a wonderful surprise.

Prayer has been like that for us. When we made the decision to start with prayer, a tremendous thing happened. Now we had a place where all the other pieces could begin coming together.

So I'd like to focus this final letter on the happy surprises of prayer.

One of these is sex at its maximum best. Sex like way out.

Martha and I have always enjoyed sex. I've liked it all. She has too. The fair, the good, the better. But after we began praying together, sex for us took off like super. And today after thirty-five years I can tell you one thing Roger might find interesting—we think great prayer is the way to great sex!

We've read the manuals, the picture books on how-to, the best sellers. The sensuous this, the sensuous that, and everything you always wanted to know. (Only we didn't really want to know *that* much. Some of the fun for us has been discovering things together.) But after reading, hearing, seeing all these highly recommended goings-on, we have decided something. Nobody, but nobody has it as good as we have it!

Why? Because—say it one more time—when we began praying together, our sex life took off like super.

Which says what? What it says to the two of us is that *sex at its best is spiritual!*

Here's a story I think you'll like and I know Roger will.

Martha and I were leading a seminar for Episcopal priests and their wives. We were explaining that for us bodies seem to blend better when souls are blending. Then, right in the middle of our presentation, one lit-up little lady raised her hand and asked for the floor. Whereupon she broke us up with this, "I can just see him now. The minute we get home, he'll rush me into the bedroom and say, 'Let us pray.'"

I hope he didn't. But I also hope they've discovered by now that the greatest sex is spiritual first.

But this wasn't the only happy surprise which came our way with prayer. As we began to pray, suddenly another serendipity. Or a lot of them! We began to see wonderful new qualities in each other we'd never seen before. Great things we'd overlooked. Little mysteries unraveled. Fresh insights. Sparkling new discoveries—and all of these still going on.

Most of us would like to believe we have a lot of good

things in us somewhere. Sure, we're somewhat tarnished now. But wasn't it nice in the original?

We'd also like to think we married somebody with considerable potential. Chances are we sold our mate on that possibility. We were somebody special and so were they. But many couples lose this "I'm-somebody-special, you're-somebody-special" feeling. As the marriage wears on, the negatives take over and the beauty wears away.

Is it really that the nice part's gone forever? Or is it merely buried under trivia? If that's how it is, then what every couple needs is some way to keep their focus on the best.

Prayer can do that for you too.

Sometimes prayer is like the quiet moving of a hand to draw aside some grasses. See? Here is a path we've never seen before.

Sometimes prayer is like a small voice calling and waiting. Anybody in there? Anybody wanting to be discovered? Anyone looking for me?

Then sometimes prayer is like a mighty bulldozer rolling over stubborn obstacles. Moving boulders aside. Clearing a way.

But whatever else prayer is, prayer at its best is *the great unifier!*

That's how it's been for us.

So if I could wish for you and Roger just one wish, this would be it: that you might begin praying together in a way which makes sense to you.

Why do I wish you this above every other wish?
I wish you this because I know from experience—

The more a husband and wife make friends together
with God,
The greater He makes their friendship for
each other.